Crossing the Same River

PATRICIA GOEDICKE

The University of Massachusetts Press
Amherst, 1980

Copyright © 1980
The University of Massachusetts Press
All rights reserved
Library of Congress Catalog Card Number 79–18809
ISBN 0–87023–287–8 (cloth), 0–87023–288–6 (paper)
Printed in the United States of America
Library of Congress Cataloging in Publication Data
appear on the last page of this book.

ACKNOWLEDGEMENT

The author would like to acknowledge the inestimable encouragement and advice most particularly of M. Cameron Grey; of the Poetry Board of the University of Massachusetts Press, especially of Rosellen Brown and John Engels; and, as always, of her husband, Leonard Wallace Robinson.

"For Walt Whitman" first appeared in *Big Moon*; "The People Gathering Together," "Greyhound" (here titled "Chihuahua") and "Crossing the Same River" first appeared in *New Letters*; "All the Princes of Heaven" and "The Rings of All That Is Possible" first appeared in *The American Poetry Review*; "In This Fog" first appeared in *Three Sisters*; "Like Animals" first appeared in *Waves*; "What the Maps Don't Mention, the Directions Never Say," "Horse" and "The Same Slow Growth" first appeared in *The Chariton Review*; "Making a Double Angel" is reprinted by permission from *The Hudson Review* (Summer 1979), copyright © 1979 by Patricia Goedicke; "In the Hope of Whose Return" and "Hot Flash" first appeared in *The Massachusetts Review*; "The Arrival" first appeared in *The Missouri Review*; "In the Ocean" was first published in *Tangled Vines*, edited by Lyn Lifshin (Boston: Beacon Press, 1978); "Though It Is Hard / For Sons" and "When Everything Is Done" first appeared in *Colorado State Review*; "What You Are Doing Here" was originally published in *The Ohio Review*; "Surrounded by Sadness, Escaping," "For Rose," "One More Time" and "Over Our Dead Bodies" first appeared in *Three Rivers Poetry Journal*, copyright © 1979 by Three Rivers Press; " 'Illness as Metaphor' " was originally published in *Harper's*.

Once again, for Leonard

CONTENTS

FOR WALT WHITMAN

Whatever it was to you,
    Finally I think I am only one blade of it,
        Tiny, infinitesimally

Also I think there is nothing very unusual about my life
    Or most people's:

Climbing the steepest face of the mountain
    Struggling to go up

Even as the dirty seesaw tips
    Slowly, irrevocably
        Down

Any one of the world's giants could step on me
    And never notice

Even if I cried out, in a cracked voice
    Under the rubble of the earthquake
        Among the dying cattle who would hear?

Not that there is anything so unextraordinary, either
    About my comings and goings:

It is just that there are so many of us,
    Each sword single,
        Each miniscule life . . .

Therefore to my mnd it is more a matter
    Of quiet roots, of connections,

Of speaking out, loud
    Or just soft enough
        For a few friends to hear

The beautiful names of all those
    Who eventually will but must not
        Entirely disappear.

CROSSING THE SAME RIVER

THE PEOPLE GATHERING TOGETHER

For all over the earth I can see them,
In every city and town
The people gathering together,

Sailing the dark waters
In great glowing patches of brightness,
Islands of floating flowers.

Once a week they swing
And dip and bend together,

Garlands of party-going faces
Wallowing in the troughs
Or high up on the crests

Refusing to think about the feet
Dangling beneath them,

The long wavering roots
Loose now, forever

They are as dazzlingly brave
And brilliant as coats of arms,

All week they work hard,
Each in the boat of himself commands
As much of the ocean as he can

So that thinking of it I could weep,
For now none of us knows where he is going
Any more than he ever did,

There are these huge distances between us,
Over the blank, heaving waves,
The vast trenches of the sea

Therefore we stick to the surface,
Floating along like huge colonies of water lilies

Whether it is Paris or London
Or a primitive tribe in New Zealand

All over the earth we keep coming together,
We keep giving each other these parties,
These heartbreakingly beautiful parties.

ALL THE PRINCES OF HEAVEN

First it is only the sense of sunlight
Creeping up over the dunes

Darkness is beginning to pale
Imperceptible sounds

In every corner of the house there are shiftings
Minute, barely distinguishable

The delicate slow tide rises
Out on the long marshes

Something is running through the tall grass
Crinkling it with excitement

Inside it is as if they were moving furniture
The heavy velvet of the couch
Blunders over to the window

The crisp curtains are beginning to breathe
Fronds of your hair sweep
Back and forth along the floor

Out on the porch of your thighs
Sandpipers flicker, with their little feet

From one fiber to the next
The flat wooden planks are beginning to swell

Now the seagulls are impatient, mewing
And flapping their wide wings,

Turning your quiet abdomen into a loud
Fourth of July day crowd

With flags waving, people
Jostling each other in the street

Your breasts are beginning to ache,
They are turning into Scylla and Charybdis

But softer, with hearts of butter,
Nipples of pure cream

Your teeth open and close like the jaws
Of a ravenous whale but gentle,
Rolling in its own sweet wake

The inner and outer lips are turning purple
Stretching themselves like a child sucking

The agitated motion of the round pilings
On either side of the dock increases

Waves slap back and forth
Both buttocks are jerking

The white galaxies of night
Inhabit the day, in a trance

The orange prow of the ship appears
Over the horizon it shoves its way
Across the smooth sheets

Shooting stars and colored streamers
And twenty-one gun salutes

All the princes of heaven come
Leaping onto the land,

Exploding together into dawn
The earth shakes itself to pieces,

In the hot arms of the sun
The sides of the waiting wharf heave
Up to the sky and then down.

IN THIS FOG

And suddenly it is as if the wing of an ant
Had whisked away the world.

Ashen, weightless,
The two of us, offstage

Are speechless,
Whispering to each other the way the trees

Shell us in shadow like fans,
Like fringed fingers caress,

Weave us into a breathing frieze
Until we become all air, air

And lighter than air we move
With winged tentative feet

Onto the stage at last,
As the footlights finally begin to flare

Without knowing it we begin to chatter
And stumble, forgetting our lines until

With blurred faces, like rowboats in gray,
With a soft shock we bump

Belly to belly like June bugs we fall
Into each other, into the blaze of day.

LIKE ANIMALS

Over her like a dog
Muscular, tricky, neat

And she under, oh under
Nuzzling the nipple of the prick,
The shaggy brush of the balls

In the depths of summer
In the heat
In the red shadows of the bedroom

His belly like the ceiling
Arms and legs like doorposts

And she brown as the floorboards
Beneath him, jiggling like a pup

In the muddle of their bodies
Grappling for each other's souls

They are feeding on each other so fiercely
They are barely able to speak:

Locked in the cave of the self
They are all alone, they are lonely

Loneliness spreads like a hole in their chests
Wheezing for breath, in darkness

Like a bone stuck in a beast's craw
In the kitchen it is a brown shadow,
A whiff of sad air . . .

Nevertheless, between them
Every once in awhile there is a quick flashing,
A sort of gurgling song:

With the bloated golden guts
Of turtle, snake, swan

With fine, spirited fingers
And nimble, intelligent feet

In a whir of mischievous wings
They cling to each other like animals

And oh it is sweet, it is sweet.

5

WHAT THE MAPS DON'T MENTION, THE DIRECTIONS NEVER SAY

But who knows where we're going?
I am thinking, perhaps
That you are thinking
Maybe . . .

Today, in the air
There was a hint,
The quiver of your
Glance

Therefore I brush my teeth,
Clean my breath
For you only but say nothing.

Of course I would like to speak,
But who knows where we're going?

Rain
Walks across the roof,

Like two peaches,
Two plums
Wrapped in a cockleshell bed

I read,
You read
As usual but underneath
Something is tugging at the boat,

Words in the shy corners
Of both our mouths wait,
Wait to be shown the way . . .

Then, in the darkness, crisp
And brisk as winter, our clean
Fragrant pajamas slide
Somewhere out of sight

But who could have known
Before, you

Like a bright ski-jumper
Yellow as the sun would leap
Into my arms like water, like snow, like ice

Stiff as feathers our words would drop
With every other intelligence
Flashing like scales from our eyes,

The flowers of the rain would open,
Like two jubilant seagulls we would fly

Far out over the diamond,
The trackless circle of the ocean.

MAKING A DOUBLE ANGEL

I will lie down here in the snow.
So.
In Edgewater
By the sea
I will open my coat out
On either side
Like a magic carpet,
The snow will rise
Great white poufs of it
To soften
Your descent? No
You stand above,
Unbuttoning
Your fly to my raised skirt
And fall like a giant tree
Or like the thunderbolt
You are
On top of dark me
Making a double angel
Our woolen clothes
At night
Like thick wings
Thrash,
Languorously
Kissing snowflakes
Away
With white eyebrows
From smooth cheeks
Halos of hair
Rise
For the moon's behind
The oak tree,
Your lovely prick
Dangles a huge
Shining star
Falling, yes
But I catch it
In my red mitten
For nothing changes,
Nothing melts

In memory
No rats squeak
Above us,
On the bridge
Cars keep
Slicing by,
Roaring through the dark
Their prying headlights
Ignorant of us
Two children playing
This one moment
Out of heaven
Even the snow supports us.

IN THE HOPE OF WHOSE RETURN

1

But caught in the family Volkswagen with you
Raging at me as you drive,

Myself retaliating, sometimes even
Initiating, the seats are so close together

Our luggage, packed in back
Keeps looming at us,

Telling us to shut up

Also the traveling kitchen, the first-aid kit
For emergency use only. . . .

But this is an emergency!

Neither of us can get out
Even though the windows are wide open,

With air hurtling through them
Like a hurricane in a cage,

Even though our words
Tear at each other like fighting birds

In such tornadoes of misery
I'm flooding the upholstery with my tears,

Beating on the armrest, swearing
Clawing at my own skin

While you like an angry blue jay
Tyrannical, in dizzy circles

Keep frightening me with pronouncements
Over and over of ruin, calamity

You're leaving me tomorrow . . .

2

So in the cycles of such wars
The car almost leaves the road

But doesn't, for cooped up here together
This intimacy is our own choice

Boiling and sputtering down the highway
In whatever fury with each other, yes

We'd rather be here than out there,

Sliding along in a huge station wagon
So silently, and swift

Smug, self-satisfied, indifferent
With perfect dispositions, controlled

Either we'd turn into heroes and heroines
Larger than life, and shinier

Carefully streamlined and polished
But desperately dreaming, in our separate seats

Of green lights flashing, eyes
Glittering at us from the far ends of the world

For here, at least, we remember,
(How close we are, how close)

Incestuous as twins, symbiotic
Locked in our steel womb

Strapped down by seat belts
Eating into our flesh,

By tongues like razors, like knives
Cutting each other's guts out

And then *explaining* them to each other
As if this were some sort of anatomy lesson,

This marriage is a live cadaver,
Like Plato's egg, seems doomed to separate

3

But will not, listen, but *will not:*

For as much as we choose anything, choose
Seeming self-destruction, choose

To lose ourselves in the familiar,
The chafing arms of each other

Surely the responsibility is ours

For every part of it,
The whole confused body
Of the cross we make together,

From side to center to side

Our wild outstretched wings
May hurl themselves in and out

As far from peace as they can get

But this agony, this torment
Is ours also, remember

Just as surely as we once chose

And keep on choosing it, the mothering
And all fathering eye of the storm

Where we first met, and embraced
Like doves balancing in air,
In the risky middle of our lives

Where the white feathers of our fingers
Clasp each other in a cathedral
Electric, full of the joyful calm

That began everything,
In the hope of whose sure return

So suddenly peaceful
And so unexpectedly gay

We keep together forever, no matter
How often we are swept away.

THE ARRIVAL

Luggage first, the lining of his suit jacket dangling
As always, just when you'd given up hope
Nimbly he backs out of the taxi

Eyes nervously extending, like brave crabs
Everywhere at once, keeping track of his papers
He pilots himself into the home berth

Like a small tug in a cloud of seagulls
Worries flutter around him so thick
It takes him some time to arrive

And you wonder if he's ever really been happy:
When the blue eyes blur
And stare out to sea

Whether it's only a daydream
Or a long pain that silences him
In such gray distances

You'll never know, but now
Turning to you, the delicate mouth
Like a magician

Is curious, sensitive, playing tricks,
Pouting like a wise turtle
It seems he has a secret

With the driver,
With the stewardess on the airplane
So that even when he opens his arms

When the warm voice surrounds you,
Wraps you in rough bliss,
Just before you go under

Suddenly you remember:
The beloved does not come
From nowhere: out of himself, alone

Often he comes slowly, carefully
After a long taxi ride
Past many beautiful men and women

And many dead bodies,
Mysterious and important companions.

IN THE OCEAN

At first my mother would be shy
Leaving my lame father behind

But then she would tuck up her bathing cap
And fly into the water like a dolphin,

Slippery as bamboo she would bend
Everywhere, everywhere I remember

For though he would often be criticizing her,
Blaming her, finding fault

Behind her back he would talk about her
All through our childhood, to me and my sister,

She rarely spoke against him

Except to take us by the hand
In the ocean we would laugh together

As we never did, on dry land

Because he was an invalid
Usually she was silent

But this once, on her deathbed

Hearing me tell it she remembered
Almost before I did, and she smiled

One more time to think of it,
How, with the waves crashing at our feet

Slithering all over her wet skin

We would rub against her like minnows
We would flow between her legs, in the surf

Smooth as spaghetti she would hold us
Close against her like small polliwogs climbing

All over her as if she were a hill,
A hill that moved, our element

But hers also, safe
In the oval of each other's arms

This once she would be weightless
As guiltless, utterly free

Of all but what she loved
Smoothly, with no hard edges,

My long beautiful mother
In her white bathing cap, crowned

Like an enormous lily

Over the brown arrow of her body,
The limber poles of her legs,

The strong cheekbones, and the shadows
Like fluid lavender, everywhere

In a rainbow of breaking foam

Looping and sliding through the waves
We would swim together as one

Mother and sea calves gliding,
Floating as if all three of us were flying.

Men cry
So seldom

It is a painful
Relief

To see them:

Though it is hard
For sons

Seeing a grown man
Broken

Wrenched like a nutcracker
Over somebody's shoulder

Lip twisted, snarling
Like a lion

Tears battering the white face

They may break down
Others with them

Or they may learn to walk
In wide nervous circles

Not touching,
Carefully

Around their own sons

Only in darkness
At theaters will they give in

One of them I know
At least once

Remembered:
Waking, I found him weeping

For the great gap that lies waiting

Another I did not see
But he told me

All the way into exile
With his twin sons

All three wept
Continuously

For many days,
Softening

Under a green rain

Helplessly they sat
Like women, some would say

This relief was enormous

WHEN EVERYTHING IS DONE

And now it is the artists who come walking
Lonely as athletes, composed

Each settled in his own skin,

But strolling into the arena
From all directions, at twilight

They come to us out of a solitude
Few know

For though they will never admit it
They are as modest as athletes,

As terrified also.

No wonder they move slow
Across the green fields

Wrapped in a strange silence, and swimming
Dust motes make gold cowls around them

Leaning into their steps like flagpoles
Or priests, swinging their heavy robes

Making their magical signs
Against the far mountains

It is difficult for them to greet us
With their hands tucked in their pockets

For what they have been doing out there
In the camps, in the rented rooms

What they have been doing is a secret
Sometimes even from themselves

And it may not work:

Leaving their long lines behind them
Confidently they step forward

But standing on the edge of success
Or failure, no matter,

As they attempt to play for us,
When everything is done

Really they feel like stray dogs
Waiting for the game to begin

Just like the rest of us, they can't help it,
They have staked all their lives on this one.

WHAT YOU ARE DOING HERE

But stepping into the spare room of your life,
The one that has been empty
Until now

What to do with it is the question:
You asked for it, after all

Now you're finally here
About to explain yourself

There is a sort of rearrangement
Of silence.

Everything's looking at you, *help*
What do you do next

You turn your head around
Very gently, you're not going to lose it
This time

What you are doing here

You stare back at everything
Carefully

The gray boulders of the fireplace
The braided peninsula of the rug

Beached on the bare stone floor
The black Steinway, the hush

Open throated but still
What's going on here

You feel like you're underwater

Speaking volumes but sentenced
To slow, ponderous motion

Eye level with the waists of the trees
All the corners of space

Contract themselves into this one room
Low ceilinged, like a cave

Bushes scratch at the windows
All that has gone before
Is looking in at you

But standing over you like giraffes,
Elegant columns to the sky,

The sleeves of the evergreens are heavy,
The hinges of the house are tall

Packed in the aisles of the trees

The snow falls like applause
Muffled, in white gloves

The world is waiting for you to explain
Whether for yourself or others

Even though you try to ignore it
The bayberry candle wavers
Dark green in its socket

It soothes you, it sits you up
Opposite the straight-backed chair in the corner . . .

Well, is there an explanation
Or not?

Certainly it is past time,
But whatever you'd say would be wishes

And really you'd prefer to be quiet,
Like the mute jaws of the piano,
The plain rug on the floor . . .

One false step and you may slip
Backwards into busyness forever!

But there's no escaping it,
Next to the window there's a Greek statue
Secondhand, left behind

Dark browed, delicately sweet
But slightly out of proportion,

Whether it is to be filled up or presented
To someone unknown, an offering

She's holding a bronze bowl in her hands
Awkwardly, looking away from it
In supplication.

SURROUNDED BY SADNESS, ESCAPING

for my sister, Jean-Marie McKenna Cook

But once more you are off,
Wearing the mantle of yourself

Like an invisible shadow

The quick hood your eyes peer out of,
The soft bush of your hair

Haloing you, your glance

Blue as the flash of wings,
Nervy as crickets, brisk

Crowds fall away from you, tall

Striding through them like a knife,
Moses parting the Red Sea

Of the problems we hurl at you, the troubles
All the anxieties . . .

And though there are narrow shadows pinned

Like sharp feathers, like nails
Uneasy, at the back of your eyes

You keep our attention where you want it:
Between us but not against us

Your long legs are powerful
But delicate also,

Beneath the tentative shoulders

The small breasts, shy as rabbits
Hide themselves under the smart clothes

You flourish at us like flags,

Waving your frail hands at us
Like tiny mirrors, as if you were a magician

Or a Byzantine madonna, smiling

With all her sorrow flattened,
Forever calm, in gold leaf

Surrounded by sadness, escaping
From us but also for us

Though the walls of your life are crumbling
Though the shimmering veils you are wrapped in
Barely protect you from your own pain

Nevertheless you keep talking,
The intricate honey of your voice

Gaily, with its crisp accents
Enchants us all with story
After marvelous story,

Like Scheherazade's hostages shining
Long after you have left us they remain.

CHIHUAHUA

For sometimes I think I am not a car but a bus
And not a Greyhound but a Chihuahua
Second-class, Mexican, hairless.

Lambs, pigs, people
Like parts of myself, stumbling
Inch up and down the aisle

But wheeling around mountains I hold on
To all my hopes, my passengers
Search the highway ahead . . .

Whizzing through beds of flowers,
Flying across deserts, ignorant
Stopping and starting
Where are we going? Inside

Galaxies of men women and children
Wave from the portholes of my pupils

For the women inside me are my rubber tires
Milking me, milking me
Back to the playpen, the huge breasts

For the children inside me are no strangers
In the West, in the South, in the North
Flying the same flag

For wherever I go I have been there already
From one filling station to the next

For the people inside me are a logjam
Of golden lumberjacks, whales in schools
Each with the same shining face:

The world's open house like an army
Surging up the passage to unseat me:

Pouring through Washington, Chihuahua, Veracruz
Crowding my corridors with bedazzled flowers

Sunfaced, moonfaced, waving from every door
Heading for new horizons where we've been before.

FOR ROSE

May not be tough enough for most men but he
Is many throated, rich, with lights

Carving beautiful red palaces

Wherever he is, in flannels
Or dungarees, picking himself up

Strong as the footsteps of a mountain

Inside the honeycombed globe of his head
Whole landscapes appear like magic,

The pieces of his life open out

On the pillow next to me there's a garden
Full of excitement, the hum

Of a hundred live birds

That soar like arrows or chirp
Sassy as sparrows in the dust,

Red-breasted, flashing back and forth

Out of the intricate depths,
The complicated corridors of his body

The idea of fire emerges,
Scarlet petal upon petal,

Fold upon fold of it like an overcoat,
Like a deep red heart beating

Secretly, in and out,

For if there are worms within he conceals them,
As a proud emblem he appears

Carnation colored, triumphant
Blazoned on a dark ground

For his anger cuts like a sword
In all directions laying waste

But swifter than lightning, as soon over
For the sake of everyone around him,

For the sake of the children next door

The delicate leaves of his lips curve,
Smiling their wise, archaic smile

For his courage is a beehive
Many-chambered, full of fragrance

To protect the innocent in velvet,

In the odor of summer flourishing
Like scented linen, like honey

His gaiety pours over everything,
Like a small satyr, on his toes

As clumsy as he is graceful,
Pirouetting on the lawn

Fearlessly, flexing his muscles
His fingers are a network

Stretching far and near

The heat of his hand is like warm earth
That has been soaking in the sun for years.

for Leonard Wallace Robinson

HORSE

for Pat Grean

That day we buried your son
O wild eyed

Wild gaunt horse
Stalking down the aisle

Lean flagpole
Reaching

Face stained red
Hollow blue pupils

Bent under tough eyebrows
Like leather

Body at half-mast
Struggling
Rags flapping in air

Yes there was a horse

Grief was digging at it
Kicking at it with its heels

Into abandoned craters
Cemeteries away

We thought we would never see you again

But you came back
One day, with the sound

Of trumpets, wild
Comfortable laughter

You held our hands
In the dark

By the side of the dark sea

You took us walking
Calmly, in the park

Showing us the leaves
Turning green, rooted

Once again, explaining
Which plants to pull up

And which not, covering
Everything for winter

You did not learn to ride that horse
For nothing

"ILLNESS AS METAPHOR"

for Susan Sontag

But somewhere outside Washington, in the crowded flat-
lands of science
I know you're lost, I'm terrified, all night long
In the steel cabinets of the dream I'm rifling the file
cabinets
In a basement full of barbed wire I'm trying to find out
who's inside
Besides typewriters and statistics, the final solution to
everything,

Like a drab spy with my bicycle leaning against the wall
outside
I'm trying to get to you before they do,
I know they only want to be helpful but I want them to be
careful,
I know this is not really Ravensbruk,
They would never consciously use us as guinea pigs

But you're lost, and I'm lost, and the poor everywhere,
And though I agree, in this century it is certainly
irresponsible
Even to suggest that cancer is anything but superficially
similar to a world
So sick it may not ever be able to cure itself,
The nightmare keeps coming back, comparisons

Proliferate like death, in dreams the metaphors we make
Pursue us everywhere, the unpurged images of each day
Cram themselves into the portmanteau of perfectly
ordinary words
Incarnate in bloody flesh, that agonized cipher reason
Alone can never analyze, even by onionskin turned brown,

For the data banks are too full, overflowing with breasts,
colons
Mutilated arms, legs, faces
Several pairs of ovaries and millions of gaunt babies
Starving, covered with flies, in test tubes or merely black.
In political theory or philosophy this may be confusing
the issue

But in the cataclysm of now
Who cares about later? Really and truly and forever

The spirit's interned in the body
For the duration, though the Brothers are waiting for us,
    they swear
Surely some country will grant us immunity

Wouldn't you think, society's not that interconnected,
    is it?
Well but unless you're utopian, even the latest miracle's
Endless, though the name changes, the disease
Remains the same, so why do you look at me like that,
    behind bars

In the damp nightsweats motionless as the radioactive
Needle drips like a time bomb through your veins but
    listen,
Why should a mere figure offend? Under the infrared
Metaphysical lamps it's easy to break the code: in this
    darkness
I'm just calling a concentration camp a concentration
    camp.

HOT FLASH

1

The news at first is nothing:

A few heated incidents
(Unusual for the time of year)

Are reported to General Brain, casually
And you ignore them, for the most part

It's easy to stay calm,
Keep cool, rise above it

Putting the whole thing in perspective
According to the A.M.A.

It's only a minor disturbance,

But the first skirmish leads to another
And another and another and another

Then you begin waking
In the middle of the night you discover it,

Mad Lieutenant Gland
Keeps sending out crazy commands

And you can't believe it, for one thing
You're much too young, and besides

What have you done to deserve *this*?

The jammed messages keep going out
And doubling back on themselves, in a panic

You keep thinking you can stop it,
But the command post itself is burning

(Your hairdresser cries out, "My dear
Your whole head is on fire!")

Even as you report it
Over the sizzling wires to your family

The top of your head is smoking,
Each individual hair fumes

Scarlet, you blink apologies
Or shriek swear words, alternating

Between fury and despair

2

Though no one notices but yourself
And a few psychologists, who insist

It's merely temporary, a condition
You should accept with relief

As the outward and physical sign
Of ultimate sexual peace . . .

But how do they know the agony
Who've never experienced it, each time

The dazzling waves of battle
That utterly overwhelm you

Like blue litmus paper turning,
Seeping through every vein

Searing you with the memory

Of whenever you were found out
Or not found out, for whatever sin, no matter

Even though it's usually nothing

But a change in temperature, a shift
In the molecules of air around you

If everyone *agrees* it's nothing
How speak of it, in public

Slithering back and forth
Restlessly, roaming the moist valleys

Of a body that *must* be punishing you
For some reason but for what?

They keep telling you it gets better

But iridescent as silk
White hot, heavily sweeping

From one battlefield to the next

In the blind glare of rockets
Bursting all over your skin

Slowly the tide goes out
And then comes in again

3

For if it gets better it gets worse:

No matter what they say
In the middle of even the mildest heat wave

Nobody, not even the doctors
Can talk about anything else:

Not every woman suffers from it
But after a certain age

The roots of your hair may drip
Water may stand in your ears

Pools of it collect
In your navel

And what's worse
(*What's* worse?)

Somehow it feels like shame, for instance
Why are you so irritable

Then in a rage
At nothing

O thus, O thus

Tossed every which way
Nearly every hour

Slides smooth and slick
And slimy as melted butter

Out from under your clothes,
Off the flowers, off the dinner plates

In a mad clay colored trickle
Runs away down the street

And you're left cooling your heels,

Clothes plastered to a body
Slippery as wet soap

Everywhere, even the backs of your knees
Which you keep investigating, amazed . . .

4

But the house itself remains

And you're inside it, helpless,
Waiting for the next attack.

Even though you know it's boring
You keep thinking about it

Over and over and over,
But what else is there to do?

Physical though it is, and trivial
As everyone agrees

Suddenly the heat rushes
From deep inside to a surface

Feverish as a secondhand hot plate

The coils of your stomach glow
Like somebody's electric burner

For no reason you're in Hell,
Your whole body is a firing line

Though they hunt the recalcitrant headcold
With all the money they command

The doctors keep telling you this is nothing
And they offer you nothing

But heavy tranquilizers, or worse
Draconian hormones, incendiary

Surrounded by invisible enemies,

Bombarded by napalm you cry out,
Frantically you try to stop it

Yourself, speaking to yourself in whispers
As if it were your fault

But struggling against it, enraged

However hard you try
You can't help it, you're a flashfire

Someone else has ignited.

Wiping sweat from your eyes
In the middle of January as if it were July

You're barely able to think,
To keep your head above water,

You can't help mentioning it to everybody,
You try not to complain but you do . . .

5

And then it's all over:

Just as they said, the pain
Vanishes, even the memory of it

Ten times a day
Or twenty

In two minutes
Or five

All at once you're shivering
As the salt sweat evaporates

Shaking like uncooked rice
Jumping in a tin bowl

On top of a mountain, exposed
Just like everybody else

For what does it matter, in the long run
What did you do *not* to deserve this?

After a certain age

You're not alone, it's the same
For everyone, almost the same horror

Even for doctors, the same indignities
In the blast furnace of our lives

In the gas ovens of our bodies
Everything about growing old

Is only a long preparation
For the cold.

THE SAME SLOW GROWTH

1

So that now, in the middle of the newest nightmare
The hospitals are filling up

In the strange proliferating seepage
Of cell upon cell, the fallout
Of the beautiful wildflowers of the atom,

In the bloodstream of the whole world
The diseased lymphatics float

2

Even as far south
As here, in Mexico City,
In this hospital waiting room

The latest victims are sitting
Like blown fuses, stiff
With dull, glazed eyes

So that I feel dead, already
This room is a morgue

Except for the woman next to me,
The one who reminds me of you, Mother

Just before you died, fighting
The same slow growth

That brings us all together, nowadays
More and more and more of us

3

Here in the radiotherapy room, myself
In a Boston skirt and blouse

And the woman next to me, with her brown skin,
Stuffed into her hospital gown
Like a bundle of broken pottery,

Her feet bare but sweating
In the cold, in secondhand shoes

Even when a child comes into the room, Mother
A little girl
Butting into her side like a goat

In the sharp cave of her body
She keeps the pain to herself, she says nothing

4

Nor is there anything I can say
In my poor Spanish but smile

And she smiles back, it is strange
In this defeated room

With such arrogance, such a concentration
Of utterly impersonal curiosity in her eyes

5

I cannot believe it:
Though the mute hands are gnarled

There is an air about her
Purer than ice, and glittering

While the city in its confusion
Flourishes all around her, while science

In the name of progress heaps
Injury upon injury upon her

6

Though the village she comes from is a backwater
High in the mountains where machines
And doctors hardly come

Nevertheless she is calm,
She is full of a huge amusement

Flickering behind the pain
And stoical gaze like fire

7

Like a ramrod of electricity
Humming with energy, alive

Whenever anything happens
She braces herself to meet it, Mother

With all her forces drawn up
She looks around her like a wildcat

Gingerly she keeps watch, alert
As the last soldier at the pass.

IN THE WAITING ROOM

But still, carrying my illness to the hospital
Everyday, carefully
As if it were a rare gift

I think I am something special,
I want everyone to pity me, to exclaim . . .

But lost in the hubbub on the main floor
There is so much merriment I could cry:

Among all the expensive flower arrangements
Like small hedges to conceal the truth

Upstairs there is gossip, there is nervous laughter
But downstairs it is quiet,
Outside the radiotherapy room

The patients stick together, in the half-light
Awkwardly leaning themselves against the wall

Like barnacles on a dim raft,
Defenseless as marshmallows, hunched
Stuffed into their gray hospital sacks

And shivering a little, in the cold
Feeling their frayed bandages

They nod but they do not speak,
The thin man with the moustache,
The woman in dark glasses

Sitting on the edge of pain
They absolutely refuse to share my grief

And suddenly it occurs to me,
In all honesty they are only interested in their own,
There is nothing special about it,

Settling uneasily among them
I stop poking at myself, oddly
But finally relieved, at home.

PRINCESS

For once they had decided on the second operation
They really did treat me like a Princess

Except that I was barefoot
In the middle of the great hall

And everyone else was in riding boots
I could not turn my head, I was kept waiting

Among the tall pillars, in the gloom
The stone columns like a forest

Till the horses came cantering,
Their hooves clattering up the aisle

And all the doctors dismounted,
They covered their grinning mouths

While my friends waved good-bye they began stripping me,
In the vast amphitheater I was the center of attention,

All eyes turned to me,
My slightest motion . . .

And afterwards, when my 3 ladies in waiting took me
    to the bathroom
Respectfully they waited but they were quite firm about it,

They told me my name was Princess,
Because I could not escape

They kept saying it, tying me up
With smooth plastic ribbons they attached me to a tube

Also they kept on petting me and caressing me
Even when I raged at them and threw tantrums

For I could do nothing wrong, the royal Will
Must be expressed, because of the operation

They had me where they wanted me,
Even my friends felt it,

When they were allowed to visit me
They stared at me as from an ice floe

But then, when they understood,
Instantly they began coming and going,

They treated me like real royalty,
In the warmth of their regard

Grass began to spring up
In the middle of the marble floor

Feeling their ordinary breath calling me, soft as the wind
My soul came and sat at the edges of my skin.

ONE MORE TIME

And next morning, at the Medical Center
Though the X-Ray Room swallows me whole,

Though cold crackles in the corridors
I brace myself against it and then relax.

Lying there on the polished steel table
I step right out of my body,

Suspended in icy silence
I look at myself from far off
Calmly, I feel free

Even though I'm not, now
Or ever:

The metal teeth of Death bite
But spit me out

One more time:

When the technician says breathe
I breathe.

But best of all is to wake
In a little village, on a Greek island

To the ship arrived in the harbor

Overnight, unexpected
The white sigh of the sails

Come to rest, for a moment
Like a smooth swan
On a pond

The placid petals lift
And settle again, softly

There is a sense of wind
Though there is no wind anywhere,

Blossomed in the round bottle of the body
Like milkweed, like a balloon
Like a parachute to the moon

Inside you there is a transparency
As if space were a lightbulb

Somehow gathered in your stomach
And pressing against you, gently

The delicate bell of glass
Shaped like the gold ring of a harp,

Curved pane of ether
Between you and the universe

As if something had dissolved
The cramped, personal muscles

Release themselves, like water
Endlessly rippling outwards
In slow circles, from a center

One is tempted to explain as seeds,
Dark particles flung
From the dreams of the night before

But must not, only be quiet,
Forget everything, relax

Into the calm mirror of the bay
Where the rings of all that is possible

Like morning-glories are hovering,
Unfolding themselves like white wings,
Sailboats in the mouth of day.

OVER OUR DEAD BODIES

1

For your arm

Lies on my lap like a live log
Steaming mahogany, a mitten

Five roasted chestnuts
Suddenly bursting into blossom

The blaze shoots up my shoulder
And through my rib cage

Like a warm day, a wool blanket
That will never end

2

Even though the town reservoir
Turns into a mill race
Roaring down hill

And sweeping us before it
In the icy torrent gasping

Struggling to keep our heads up
In a few seconds we will drown

We will shoot over the sluiceways
Like waterlogged canoes,

Livid bellies churning,
Choking black stones

Your arm will reach out
Over our dead bodies I swear
We will reach dry land together

3

For our clasped hands
Are bedded down here

In the clay pot of our marriage
Like two zinnias, two bachelor buttons
Side by side, dreaming

Whole conflagrations of trees,
The smell of cloves like incense

Sprinkling its red petals through the air
In the furnace of the true fire

That will fuse everything into melted crystal,
One clear globe

With the sky resting in it like sapphire.

CROSSING THE SAME RIVER

For the Continuity Man splices
Scene / after scene
Together

And then throws them away / helpless
Because they keep changing

They refuse to stay the same

They will gather no moss
He insists

Nobody ever took photographs of us
As children

We have changed,
Changed entirely from the time

In the quick burst
Of a flashbulb

Someone once said
Hold still / darling
Hold still . . . .

But I will remember
And you will remember

What we said before:

No bigger than a moth's shadow
With soft shaky wings

Something in us
Persists:

From one decade
To the next / registering

However delicately / pictures
That become part of us

What each of us is
And will be

Layers of living
Accumulate

Breath after breath / no heavier
Than marsh lights

Though the skin seems
To slough off

Flakes of mica
Disappear

For every imprint
There is a negative

For every forgotten flower

Quietly closeted / somewhere
For every hand there is another

In the cloudy folds
Of the brain

Everything we have ever known

Is only waiting for its opposite
Its other half to leap

Into the positive light

Clapped in its bronze arms
And swinging

Back and forth like bells
Endlessly touching each other / out loud

The almost invisible / the one
Smallest fraction grows

Into the giant watermelon of the tongue
Banging back and forth / and spurting

Foaming / fizzing / cascading
The brilliant amber of its voice beating

Into the open marigold of a body

That stays in one place / leaving
Only to return again

In such gallant continuity
The high ancient paean
Of the bell towers of mankind

The huge metal sails vibrate
Like a hive of singing bees

The liquid notes peal
Every hour on the hour

The sweet, steadfast cells of love
Forever replacing each other / and ringing.

Library of Congress Cataloging in Publication Data
Goedicke, Patricia.
Crossing the same river.
I. Title.
PS3557.032C7   811'.5'4   79–18809
ISBN 0–87023–287–8
ISBN 0–87023–288–6 pbk.